Please return /

NATURE DETECTIVE

British Seashore

Victoria Munson

WAYLAND

First published in 2015 by Wayland
Copyright © Wayland 2015

Wayland
338 Euston Road
London NW1 3BH

Wayland Australia
Level 17/207 Kent Street
Sydney, NSW 2000

Designer: Elaine Wilkinson
Consultant: Peter Littlewood, Director,
Young People's Trust for the Environment

Acknowledgements:
Alamy 10 The Wildlife Studio; 21 Nik Taylor
Wildlife; Interpix; 30 Jack Perks; 31 Wolfgang
Polzer; 42 Steve Taylor ARPS; 43, 47
imageBROKER; FLPA 15 Steve Trewhella; Istock:
4 aristotoo; 6t northlightimages; 8 Vitaly Korovin;
16 Whiteway; 19 AtWaG; 20 ImageShopUK;
i-Spi-Photography; 26 plinney; Mantonature;
38 coastalrunner; Naturepl 29 Sue Daly;
Shutterstock: 3tl Andrew Roland; 3tr Mike Charles;
3b SusanMcM; 4t C Jones; 2r, 5t Ian Woolcock; 5b
David Hughes; 6 Stephen Rees; 8: PicturePartners;
9, 27 Bildagentur Zoonar GmbH; 11 Marco Uliana;
12 pzAxe; 13 Fokin Oleg; 14 Quan Zheng; 17 Jane
Rix; 18 24Novembers; 22 Sergei25; 24 Philip
Bird LRPS CPAGB; 25 Stephen Rees; 32 Steve
Cordory; 33 Awe Inspiring Images; 34 Copit; 36
Martin Fowler; 37 Henrik Larsson; 39 Ron Rowan
Photography; 40 Marbury; 41 C Tatiana; 44
Randimal; 45 EMJAY SMITH; 46 Rasmus Holmboe
Dahl; 48 Zadiraka Evgenii; 49 gephoto; Derek R.
Audette; 51 Emi; 52 Sue Robinson; 53 Erni; 54
V.Belov; 55 Erni; 56 Erni; 57 Mark Medcalf; 58b
Mike Charles; 63 Vilainecrevette; Artwork by Peter
Bull 7, 59. With thanks to Jim, Lily and Polly.

A cataloguing record for this title is available
at the British Library.
Dewey number: 578.7'699'0941-dc23
ISBN: 978 0 7502 9285 6
ebook: 978 0 7502 9322 8

Printed in China

Wayland, part of Hachette Children's Group and
published by Hodder and Stoughton Limited.
www.hachette.co.uk

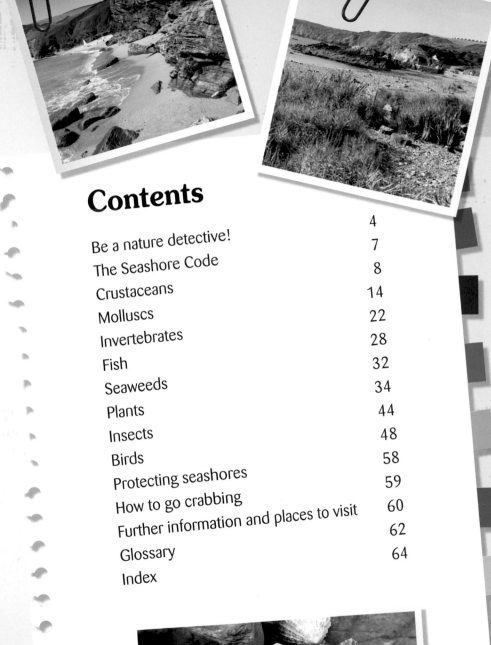

Contents

Be a nature detective!

To be a nature detective you need to be observant, patient and quiet. A lot of seashore animals are good at hiding, so you may have to spend a long time searching for them. Move slowly and carefully as sudden movements will scare the animals away.

What is the seashore?

The seashore is the point where land meets sea. Seashore can be sandy, rocky or pebbly. Shingle beaches are made up of lots of small stones. Rocky shores have many different types of wildlife living on and around the rocks. On sandy beaches there are sand dunes, shells and seaweed to spot.

Rocky shore

Lower shore

Parts of a beach

There are several parts of a beach. Each part of the shore has different types of plants and animals there. The highest part is called the splash zone, which is only made wet by the sea during very high tides or in storms. Next is the upper shore. Here, the sea covers this part of the shore during spring tides, which happen every two weeks at the time of full and new moons.

The middle part of the beach is called the middle shore. This area is always covered and uncovered by the sea. The most typical seashore plants and animals are found here. The bottom of the beach is called the lower shore and is mostly covered by shallow water.

Middle shore

Clifftop nature

Cliffs are where the edges of hills reach the sea. Clifftops are often grassy and are home to many different kinds of insects, birds and mammals. Gulls perch on ledges on a cliff-side. Kittiwakes nest in large groups on cliff sides. Guillemots lay their eggs on narrow ledges. Flowers, such as Rock Samphire and Thrift, grow on clifftops.

Cliff edges are very dangerous as they crumble easily and without warning. Always stay away from the edge.

Three million people live along the British coastline.

Tides

Twice a day, the sea moves up the shore and back down again. These movements are called tides. At high tide waves are at the top part of the beach. Low tide is when the sea is at the lowest part of the beach.

Tides are very strong and it can be dangerous to be on the beach at high tide. Before setting out to explore the seashore, check the tide times. It's best to go exploring a couple of hours before low tide. That way you can follow the tide down, so that you can explore the lower shore, and then you will notice when the tide starts to come in. The tide can rise very quickly over a flat beach. Make sure you allow plenty of time to be able to get safely to the upper shore.

Exploring rock pools

Investigating what is in a rock pool is great fun. Wear comfortable, sturdy shoes to climb over the rocks, as some shells can be sharp and seaweed makes the rocks slippery. Old trainers are ideal as they have good grip and it doesn't matter if they get wet.

Approach the rock pool slowly and quietly. You may have to look for a long time before you spot anything. Try not to let your shadow fall over the rock pool as this will make creatures hide. Lift up some small rocks to see if there are any creatures hiding there.

Seashore food chain

Every living thing depends on each other for food. This is called a food chain. At the seashore, plants, algae or plankton are at the bottom of a food chain. Mammals are usually at the top of a food chain.

The diagram on the left shows a seashore food chain. Seaweed is eaten by Sandhoppers. Crabs will eat Sandhoppers. Gulls eat Crabs.

Gull eats Crab

Crab eats Sandhopper

Sandhopper eats Seaweed

Wildlife Trusts' Seashore Code

- Don't throw things in rock pools.
- Put rocks back in the same place that you found them.
- Be gentle with animals and if you pick them up, return them to the same place that you found them.
- Don't pull seaweed off the rocks.
- Don't kick or pull limpets off the rocks.
- Don't frighten seabirds

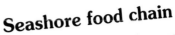

In Britain, no one lives more than 130 km (80 miles) from the coast.

Edible Crab

Scientific name: *Cancer pagurus*
Size: up to 25 cm
Habitat: Rocks and deep water on the lower shore
Food: Molluscs

The Edible Crab is noticeable by its 'pie-crust' crinkles around the edge of its shell. It has wide, dark-tipped pincers and is a reddy-pink colour. The legs are hairy and rounded.

Common Shore Crab

Scientific name: *Carcinus maenas*
Size: up to 10 cm
Habitat: Rock pools, lower and middle shore
Food: Molluscs

As its name suggests, this is the most common crab in Britain. It is a browny-green colour. All crabs have four pairs of legs and a front pair of pincers. The pincers are used to fight and catch prey. If you see a crab with just one claw, it probably lost the other one fighting.

The Common Shore Crab is also known as a European Green Crab.

Hermit Crab

Scientific name: *Pagarus bernhardus*
Size: 3.5 cm
Habitat: Sandy and rocky shores
Food: Plant and animal remains

Hermit Crabs don't have their own
shell, but live inside the empty shell of
other animals such as Whelks and Periwinkles.
Their soft body is then protected in the shell. Hard, red
pincers stick out of the shell, helping them to move and
catch food. The right pincer is larger than the left.

Sandhopper

Scientific name: *Talitrus saltator*
Size: up to 2 cm
Habitat: Sandy beaches on upper shore
Food: Rotting seaweed and dead animals

Sandhoppers always have one antenna that is longer and thicker than the other.

In early evening, large numbers of Sandhoppers can be seen jumping among the stones and seaweed looking for food.
They have large black eyes, seven pairs of legs and a short tail.
The grey-green body is divided into segments.

Sandhoppers are also known as 'Beach Fleas'.

Sea Slater

Scientific name: *Ligia oceanica*
Size: 2–3 cm long
Habitat: Rocks and pebbles on upper shore
Food: Seaweed, dead plants and animals

Sea Slaters are also known as Sea Roach or Common Slater

Sometimes hard to spot because they move so fast, Sea Slaters look very similar to a garden Woodlouse. They have two long antennae and large black eyes.

Acorn Barnacle

Scientific name: *Semibalanus balanoides*
Size: up to 1.5 cm
Habitat: Rocks on the middle to upper shore
Food: Plankton

The Acorn Barnacle is the most common type of Barnacle in Britain.

At low tide, particularly in the north of Britain, large numbers of Acorn Barnacles can be seen clinging to rocks. Their shell is grey-white with a diamond-shaped opening at the top. When the tide is out, the shell is closed, but underwater the Barnacle opens and sticks out its feathery limbs to feed.

Edible Periwinkle

Scientific name: *Littorina littorea*
Size: up to 3 cm
Habitat: Rock pools on upper or middle shore
Food: Seaweed

You can buy bags of Edible Periwinkles to eat.

This small snail has a thick, rounded shell with a sharp point on the end, although the point eventually gets worn away by the tides. The shell has grey-brown spirals and is thinly-ridged.

Laver Spire

Scientific name: *Hydrobia ulvae*
Size: 4–6 mm
Habitat: Salt marshes, mudflats, estuaries
Food: Silt and fungi

Up to 300,000 Laver Spire can be found in one square metre.

Laver Spire are snails found in large numbers on rocks and in rock pools. Small, spiral, yellow-brown empty shells can often be found on beaches. When the tide is in, Laver Spire float upside down on the surface of the water using a raft of mucus.

Laver Spires are also known as 'Mudsnails'.

Common Limpet

Scientific name: *Patella vulgata*
Size: up to 6 cm
Habitat: Rocky shores
Food: Algae

Limpet shells found on the upper shore have taller shells than those found on the lower shore.

On the underside of this grey-white, cone-shaped shell is a muscular 'foot' that the Limpet uses to move around when the tide is in. It returns to the same spot by following the mucus trail it left behind. There is sometimes a dent in the rock where the Limpet has been, because they return to the same spot so often.

Dog Whelk

Scientific name: *Nucella lapillus*
Size: up to 6 cm
Habitat: Rocky shores
Food: Molluscs

Dog Whelks were used in Anglo-Saxon times to produce purple dyes.

Related to garden snails, Dog Whelks have creamy-yellowish or light grey shells, although they can also be shades of orange, yellow, brown or black. Dog Whelks have a toothed, tongue-like structure that bores through the softened shell of other molluscs. It then paralyses and dissolves the prey and sucks it out through the hole in the shell.

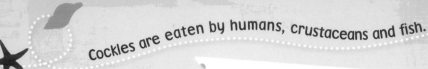

Common Cockle

Scientific name: *Cerastoderma edule*
Size: up to 5 cm
Habitat: Sand or muddy areas
Food: Plankton

The Cockle's off-white shell has ribs and circular growth lines. If you count these circular lines, you can tell how old the shell is because it grows a new line each year. Cockles can live for up to nine years. Cockle shells are tightly closed when out of the water, but underwater they open to take in food.

Common Mussel

Scientific name: *Mytilus edulis*
Size: up to 20 cm
Habitat: Rocky shores
Food: Plankton

Common Mussels are often found together in large numbers. Each has a long oval, bluish-purplish shell. The inside of the shell is smooth and pearly. Mussels close up when they are out in the air, and open when they are covered with sea.

19

Common Oyster

Scientific name: *Ostrea edulis*
Size: up to 11 cm
Habitat: Rocky shores and estuaries
Food: Plankton

The towns of Colchester and Whitstable hold Oyster festivals every year.

Common Oysters
have two rough, ridged
shells joined together. Each side
is a different size. One side is curved
and the other is flat so that they fit well together.
Inside, the shell is a shiny, smooth, pearly colour.

Pod Razor Shell

Scientific name: *Ensis siliqua*
Size: up to 20 cm
Habitat: Sandy beaches
Food: Plankton

Pod Razor Shells get their name because they look like an old-fashioned cut-throat razor.

The Pod Razor Shell is an edible shellfish. It has a large muscular foot, which it uses to help bury it deep down in the sand. Pod Razor Shells live beneath the sand and are only usually found on a beach when they are dead.

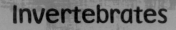

Common Jellyfish are also known as 'Moon Jellies'.

Common Jellyfish

Scientific name: *Aurelia aurita*
Size: 25 cm diameter
Habitat: Sea
Food: Plankton, molluscs, crustaceans and worms

Common Jellyfish are often found floating near the sea's edge, washed ashore or stranded in rock pools. They are domes of transparent jelly with four purplish, C-shaped markings on them. Their stinging tentacles can't hurt humans, but they use them to sting and catch prey.

Beadlet Anemone

Scientific name: *Actinia equina*
Size: 6 cm diameter
Habitat: Rock pools
Food: Plankton and small animals

One Beadlet Anemone can have up to 192 tentacles.

With their tentacles hidden away, Beadlet Anemones are jelly-like blobs attached to rocks. When their tentacles are out, they can sting their prey and drag them into their body to eat. Beadlet Anemones can be red, green or brown.

Common Starfish

Scientific name: *Asterias rubens*
Size: from 15–30 cm
Habitat: Sandy or rocky shores
Food: Mussels, cockles and barnacles

Common Starfish are an orange-brown colour. Their top side is covered in small spines. The bottom side has suckers, which they use to eat and to help them move about. If Starfish lose an arm trying to escape from a predator, they are able to re-grow them again.

Edible Sea Urchin

Scientific name: *Echinus esculentus*
Size: up to 16 cm wide
Habitat: Rocky shores
Food: Seaweed, algae and shellfish

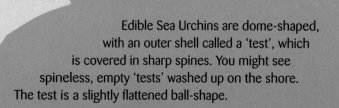

Edible Sea Urchins are dome-shaped,
with an outer shell called a 'test', which
is covered in sharp spines. You might see
spineless, empty 'tests' washed up on the shore.
The test is a slightly flattened ball-shape.

Sea Potato

Scientific name: *Echinocardium cordatum*
Size: up to 9 cm
Habitat: Lower sandy shore
Food: Organic waste

The Sea Potato is also known as a 'Heart Urchin'.

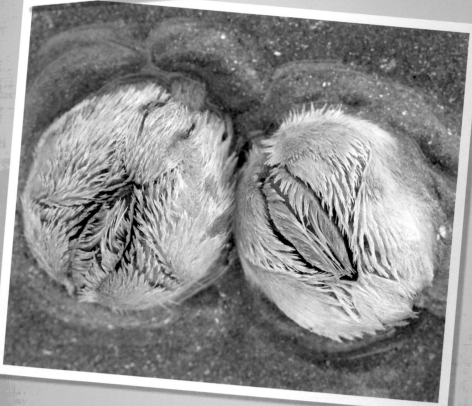

Sea Potatoes look like hairy potatoes! They are covered in light-brown spines that makes it look hairy. They usually live buried in up to 15 cm of muddy or sandy shore. The outer shell, the 'test', of the dead animal can be washed ashore in huge numbers. This heart-shaped 'test' has a very thin, fragile shell.

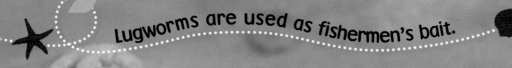
Lugworm

Scientific name: *Arenicola marina*
Size: up to 20 cm
Habitat: Sandy beaches and muddy shores
Food: Micro-organisms

Lugworms live in a U-shaped burrow under the sand. Here, they eat the sand and filter out small bits of food. Waste sand is left behind as squiggly heaps on the surface. Lugworms can live for five to six years. They look similar to Earthworms.

Lesser Weever Fish

Scientific name: *Echiichthys vipera*
Size: up to 18 cm
Habitat: Shallow waters
Food: Small fish

The word "weever" comes from an old French word "wivre", which means "dragon" or "serpent".

Venomous spikes on this fish can give you a very painful sting if you tread on them as they tend to lurk just beneath the sand. This yellowish-brown fish has a large sloping mouth, pointed snout and eyes on the top of its head. Lesser Weever Fish are only found in sandy areas on the lower shore and are mainly active at night.

Shanny

Scientific name: *Lipophrys pholis*
Size: up to 16 cm
Habitat: Rock pools
Food: Barnacles and crabs

Shannies are hard to spot because they are so well camouflaged. Their skin is green-brown with dark blotches that look like the small stones in the rock pools they are found in. They have tough teeth that they use to crack open Barnacle shells. Their body is protected by a thick layer of slime that helps them to slide between rocks.

Rock Goby

Scientific name: *Gobius paganellus*
Size: up to 12 cm
Habitat: Rock pools and shallow water
Food: Worms, crustaceans and small fish

Rock Gobies look similar to Shannies, but have more rounded heads and two distinct fins on their back. The fins underneath Gobies have suckers that help them stick to rocks so that they aren't washed away. Gobies are covered in brown and black blotches that make them hard to spot.

Gobies can lay up to 7,000 eggs at one time.

Tompot Blenny

Scientific name: *Parablennius guttorugine*
Size: up to 30 cm
Habitat: Rock pools and shallow water
Food: Anemones

This large fish has big round eyes, a large head and a thin body. It is orangey-brown, with dark brown bars on its body. It is easily recognisable by the feathery tentacles on the top of its head.

31

Bladderwrack

Scientific name: *Fucus vesiculosus*
Length: up to 2 metres
Habitat: Rocky shores

Bladderwrack is used for food and medicine.

Bladderwrack gets its name from
its rounded air 'bladders', which are
small parts full of air. The air bladders keep the
seaweed afloat. It is a dark green-brown colour and is
stronger than other green seaweeds that tear more easily.

Egg Wrack

Scientific name: *Ascophyllum nodosum*

Length: up to 2 metres

Habitat: Rocky shores

Egg Wrack sticks to rocks using a 'holdfast', which is a round, root-like growth. It has large egg-shaped air bladders, although these do not make the 'popping' sound that Bladderwrack air bladders make. It also looks more tangled than Bladderwrack. You can estimate the age of Egg Wrack by counting the bladders because they usually grow one a year.

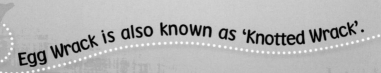

Egg Wrack is also known as 'Knotted Wrack'.

Marram Grass

Scientific name: *Ammophila arenaria*
Height: 60–120 cm
Family: Grass
Flowers: June to August

Found growing in and around sand dunes, Marram Grass is tall and spiky. The glossy thin leaves are rolled up to help it conserve water. Marram Grass has long roots that help it to find water. The roots also hold the sand in sand dunes together, which helps stop the dunes being blown away.

Sea Holly

Scientific name: *Eryngium maritimum*
Height: up to 60 cm
Family: Carrot
Flowers: July to September

With its blue-green spiky leaves, Sea Holly is easy to identify. It grows on sand dunes, rocks and shingle along the coastline. In summer, the flower heads are round and light purplish-blue. Waxy leaves help to keep in water.

Sea Campion

Scientific name: *Silene uniflora*
Height: up to 15 cm
Family: Pink
Flowers: June to September

Sea Campion grows in clumps low to the ground on shingle beaches and on clifftops. The flowers have a large bulbous bottom with white petals that are quite thick. Leaves are pointed, waxy and dark green.

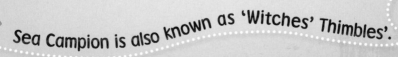

Sea Campion is also known as 'Witches' Thimbles'.

Sea Pea

Scientific name: *Lathyrus japonicus*
Height: up to 20 cm
Family: Pea
Flowers: May to August

Peas
from this
plant taste
delicious!

Found on shingle beaches,
Sea Peas have wide, oval leaves
and long, drooping purple flowers.
Flowers grow in clusters of up to nine, although
the plants don't flower until they are at least three
years old. Pea-like seeds grow in pods in late summer.

Yellow-horned Poppy

Scientific name: *Glaucium flavum*
Height: up to 90 cm
Family: Poppy
Flowers: June to September

The sap from this Poppy's stem is very poisonous!

This plant with bright yellow petals gets its name from its seed pods, which are long and curved like elephants' tusks. The Yellow-horned Poppy is a sprawling plant with thick, rough, green leaves.

Silverweed

Scientific name: *Potentilla anserina*
Height: 5–20 cm
Family: Rose
Flowers: May to August

This low-growing plant is found on sandy and shingle shores.
Its leaflets are covered in fine silvery hairs, which give the plant its
name. The small, yellow flowers look like Buttercups and have five
petals. The creeping stems look red.

In the past, Silverweed was used in shoes to soak up sweat.

Rock Samphire

Scientific name: *Crithmum maritimum*
Height: up to 30 cm
Family: Carrot
Flowers: July to September

This pretty plant has small, yellow-green flowers grouped together on flower heads. Leaves are finely branched like ferns. It is usually found growing high up on clifftops.

Thrift

Scientific name: *Armeria maritima*
Height: up to 20 cm
Family: Leadwort
Flowers: April to July

Thrift is known by many names, including 'Sea Pink', 'Rock Rose', 'Ladies' Cushion' and 'Mary's Pillow'.

This delicate plant has rounded, pink, clover-like flowers on tall, hairy stems. The leaves are long and fat and are tightly packed together forming a cushion on the ground. It is found on upper shores and cliffs.

Sea Kale

Scientific name: *Crambe maritima*
Height: up to 75 cm
Family: Cabbage
Flowers: June and July

Sea Kale forms a large, low-growing clump on sandy and shingle beaches. It has strongly smelling white flowers and large, fleshy leaves that hold in water. The stems are thick and woody. Seeds grow in pods.

Sea Kale can be cooked and eaten.

Glasswort

Scientific name: *Salicornia europaea*
Height: up to 30 cm
Family: Amaranth
Flowers: August and September

Glasswort is a thin, fleshy plant. It has upright branches with very small, stumpy leaves that are hardly noticeable. In August, tiny, thin flowers appear. Glasswort can be cooked and eaten.

Cinnabar Moth

Scientific name: *Tyria jacobaeae*
Wingspan: 3.5 cm
Habitat: Sand dunes, wasteland and meadows
Food: Ragwort

Cinnabar Moths are unmistakable with bright red stripes on a black body. The red stripes warn other insects not to eat them. They are most active at night, although they can be seen in the daytime, too.

Common Blue

Scientific name: *Polyommatus icarus*
Wingspan: 3–4 cm
Family: Blues
Habitat: Sand dunes, meadows and woods
Food: Bird's-foot-trefoil

Common Blue butterflies can be seen feeding on flowers near sand dunes. The upper side of their wings is blue, but the underside is grey-brown with orange markings and white-ringed black spots. Males have very blue upper wings, while females have a dusting of blue surrounded by brown. Common Blue caterpillars are pale green with yellow stripes.

Common Grayling

Scientific name: *Hipparchia semele*
Wingspan: 5–6 cm
Family: Browns
Habitat: Sand dunes and clifftops
Food: Grasses

This large butterfly likes
to land in sunny dry spots and
feed on grasses. It is dark brown with
orange marks and two prominent black 'eye'
spots on the forewings. The underwings are marbled
grey and brown and help to camouflage the butterfly.

Sand Digger Wasp

Scientific name: *Ammophila sabulosa*
Size: up to 2 cm
Habitat: Seashore and heathland
Food: Insects and nectar

Sand Digger Wasps have a black body with a bright orange waist.
The body is clearly divided into two segments that narrows in the middle.
They use their sting to stun caterpillars, which they drag back to their
nest. The wasps lay their eggs inside the caterpillars' bodies. When the
wasp larvae hatch, they then eat the live caterpillars.

Sand Digger Wasps are also known as 'Red-banded Sand Wasps'.

Birds

Black-headed Gull

Scientific name: *Chroicocephalus ribibundus*
Size: 44 cm
Family: Gulls
Life span: more than 30 years
Food: Worms, insects, fish and carrion

In summer, Black-headed Gulls have a distinctive black head, but for the rest of the year they have a white head with chocolate-brown stripes. They have grey wings, red legs and a white body.

Herring Gull

Scientific name: *Larus argentatus*
Size: 55–67 cm
Family: Gulls
Life span: up to 30 years
Food: Fish and scraps

Herring Gulls are large, noisy birds. They have a light-grey back and wings with white underparts. The wings are tipped with black and white. In winter, their head is streaked with grey-brown marks. For the rest of the year, the head is white. The hooked yellow bill has a red spot, which chicks tap on to tell their parents that they're hungry. The parent birds regurgitate their latest meal into the chicks' open mouths.

Common Gull

Scientific name: *Larus canus*
Size: 55–60 cm
Family: Gulls
Life span: up to 27 years
Food: Fish, invertebrates and insects

The Common Gull has grey wings, a black tail with white bars, a white head and body, and a yellow bill. Their legs have a greenish-tinge. In winter, the head has grey-brown flecks on it. Common Gulls are seen inland as well as along the coast.

Kittiwake

Scientific name: *Rissa tridactyla*
Size: 38–40 cm
Family: Gulls
Life span: up to 20 years
Food: Fish, shrimps and worms

Kittiwakes are often mistaken for other gulls. However, Kittiwakes are only seen in the summer, coming to cliff edges to breed or to feed. They have a small yellow bill, dark eyes, a grey back and white underneath with black wingtips. Their distinctive 'kittiwake' call gives them their name.

Guillemot

Scientific name: *Uria aalge*
Size: 38–54 cm
Family: Auks
Life span: 10–20 years
Food: Fish and crustaceans

Guillemots spend most of their life at sea, coming to land only to nest during the spring and summer. They have a very dark-brown back, head and bill, and a white front. The tail is short and square. They look a bit like flying penguins!

Razorbill

Scientific name: *Alca torda*
Size: 37–39 cm
Family: Auks
Life span: 10–15 years
Food: Fish such as sandeels, sprats and herrings

This sea bird has a black head, wings and back, and white underparts. It looks very similar to the Guillemot, but the Razorbill's thick, blunt beak has a white stripe on it and its tail is pointed.

Oystercatcher

Scientific name: *Haematopus ostralegus*
Size: 40–45 cm
Family: Oystercatchers
Life span: up to 15 years
Food: Worms, molluscs and shellfish

Oystercatchers are most recognisable by their long orange-red bill, which they use to prise open Cockles and Mussels. They have a black back and wings with white underparts and tail.

Ringed Plover

Scientific name: *Charadrius hiaticula*
Size: 17–19 cm
Family: Plovers and lapwings
Life span: 5–10 years
Food: Insects, crustaceans, molluscs and worms

The Ringed Plover has a brown back and wings, a black and white striped head with a brown crown and a black-tipped orange bill. It lays its eggs in a shallow 'scrape' in sand or stones lined with grass.

Curlew

Scientific name: *Numenius arquata*
Size: 50–60 cm
Family: Sandpiper
Life span: 10–20 years
Food: Worms, insects, crabs, starfish, molluscs

Curlews are a mottled light-brown colour with grey legs and a distinctive long curved bill. They are often seen searching for food among rocks or in mud. They get their name from their call which is a loud 'curloo-oo'.

Dunlin

Scientific name: *Calidris alpina*
Size: 16–20 cm
Family: Sandpiper
Life span: up to 10 years
Food: Worms, insects and molluscs

This wading bird is often seen walking slowly along the wet shore looking for food. It has a light brown back in winter, which is darker and more streaked in summer. In summer, it also has a very dark patch on its belly. Its beak is long, straight and black, useful for breaking open mollusc shells to get the food inside.

Protecting seashores

Seashores are visited by huge numbers of people and, because of this, they are under threat. Boat trips out to sea pollute the waters, people leave rubbish behind which can endanger wildlife and walkers wear away coastal paths or damage animals' habitats.

You can help

Charities, such as the National Trust or the Wildlife Trusts, look after and protect seashores. Look up their websites and support their activities. If you live near the seashore, you could join a beach-cleaning group.

If you are just visiting, find out what fun events are happening to help you learn more about the seashore.

Respect and protect

When you're at the seashore, remember to treat the environment with respect. Always leave animals and plants where you found them. Take your litter home and leave as little sign of your presence as possible.

How to go crabbing

1 Tie the bait onto a line and put it into the rockpool.

2 When you feel the line being tugged, raise it steadily and smoothly up.

3 Take a net and scoop under the crab to bring it to the surface.

4 Put the crab gently into your bucket of sea water. Don't put any more than three crabs in a bucket at a time. Keep big crabs and small crabs apart, because they will fight.

5 Don't keep the crabs out of the sea for too long. Gently put them back, preferably by hand or by lowering the bucket into the sea. Crabs can easily become stuck in a net, so if you use the net, give them time to find their way out.

6 So you don't get a nip, hold the crab by the shell on each side with your finger and thumb just behind the pincers.

Handle any animals that you find very carefully.

Further information

Places to visit

A good place to find the best beaches to visit is to look up the Blue Flag list. Every year, the cleanest beaches in Britain are awarded a 'Blue Flag' to show they have met the highest standards for quality of water and beaches. Some beaches that have achieved this recently are:

East Midlands: Mablethorpe Central, Skegness Central, Sutton-on-Sea and Cleethorpes North Promenade

East of England: Cromer, Sea Palling, Sheringham, Mundesley, Martello Bay in Clacton-on-Sea, Dovercourt Bay, Brightlingsea, Frinton-on-Sea, Southwold Pier and South Claremont Pier in Lowestoft

North East: Tynemouth Longsands, King Edwards Bay, Whitley Bay, Sandhaven

Yorkshire: North Bay in Scarborough, Whitby and Hornsea

South East: Littlehampton Coastguards, Tankerton, Hayling Island Beachlands, Sandown, Ventnor, Yaverland, Colwell, Minnis Bay, West Bay, St Mildreds, Westbrook Bay, Botany Bay, Joss Bay, Stone Bay, West Wittering

South West: Kimmeridge, Wembury, Blackpool Sands, Sandbanks, Shore Road, Canford Cliffs and Branksome Chine in Poole, Alum Chine, Durley Chine, Fisherman's Walk and Southbourne in Bournemouth, Carbis Bay, Sandy Bay, Salcombe South Sands, Swanage Central, Dawlish Warren, Breakwater, Broadsands, Meadfoot, Oddicombe.

Shoalstone Beach in Devon has a rock pool big enough to be a swimming pool. Polzeath and Portreath in Cornwall are said to have inspired the Famous Five with lots of secluded coves to explore.

Wales: Rhosilli and Broughton Bay, Gower Peninsula

Scotland: Aberdour Silver Sands and Ruby Bay

Websites

www.goodbeachguide.co.uk
The good beach guide tells you how to find the best and cleanest beaches in Britain, giving a description of each. You could register to help clean a beach with the annual 'Great British Beach Clean'.

www.mcsuk.org
The Marine Conservation Society is a charity that looks after campaigns for clean seas and shores, and saves threatened wildlife. It runs the Good Beach Guide and the 'Great British Beach Clean' campaign.

www.keepbritaintidy.org/blueflag/541
Find out which beaches have been awarded Blue Flags this year.

www.wildlifetrusts.org/rockpools
The Wildlife Trusts' website gives a list of some of the best places to go rockpooling.

www.wildlifetrusts.org/wildlife/habitats/coastal
This website tells you all about coastal habitats and why they are threatened.

https://ypte.org.uk/factsheets/seashore/the-rocky-shore
The Young People's Trust for the Environment is a charity which aims to encourage young people's understanding of the environment and the need for sustainability.
This web page tells you all about the seashore.

Glossary

air bladder pockets of air, which help some seaweeds to float

camouflage colouring on an animal that helps it to look like its surroundings

crustaceans a group of animals that have many legs and a hard body shell, such as crabs and shrimps

habitat the home of plants or animals, such as a seashore, wood or desert

high tide the highest point that the sea reaches on the shore

holdfast a root-like part used by seaweed to hold it onto rocks

insect insects have three main body parts: the head, thorax and abdomen and have six legs. They may have one or two pairs of wings.

larvae an insect after it hatches from an egg and before it changes into an adult

low tide the lowest point that the sea reaches on the shore

micro-organisms tiny animals that are so small they can only be seen through a microscope

molluscs a group of soft-bodied animals that protect themselves in shells, such as cockles and mussels

pincers the pointed claw of an animal, such as a crab

plankton tiny floating plants and animals

prey an animal hunted and eaten by another animal

sand dunes where wind has blown loose sand which has grouped together in a pile

shingle small rounded pebbles

species a group of animals that look similar and behave in the same way

spines stiff, sharp points on an animal or plant

tentacles thin, flexible parts of an animal's body that are used for grasping or moving

test the outer shell part of an animal, such as an urchin

tides the rise and fall of the sea on the seashore

venomous has a poisonous sting

Index

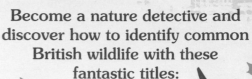